The Greatest Battles in History: The l

By Charles l

A picture of Russian soldiers advancing to the front

About Charles River Editors

Charles River Editors provides superior editing and original writing services across the digital publishing industry, with the expertise to create digital content for publishers across a vast range of subject matter. In addition to providing original digital content for third party publishers, we also republish civilization's greatest literary works, bringing them to new generations of readers via ebooks.

Sign up here to receive updates about free books as we publish them, and visit Our Kindle Author Page to browse today's free promotions and our most recently published Kindle titles.

Introduction

A picture of Russian women digging trenches to prepare the city's defenses

The Battle of Moscow

"We underestimated the enemy's strength, as well as his size and climate." – Heinz Guderian

"The savagery of that retreat is a spectacle to stun the mind." – *The New York Times*

The names of history's most famous battles still ring in our ears today, with their influence immediately understood by all. Marathon lent its name to the world's most famous race, but it also preserved Western civilization during the First Persian War. Saratoga, won by one of the colonists' most renowned war heroes before he became his nation's most vile traitor. Hastings ensured the Normans' success in England and changed the course of British history. Waterloo, which marked the reshaping of the European continent and Napoleon's doom, has now become part of the English lexicon. In Charles River Editors' Greatest Battles in History series, readers can get caught up to speed on history's greatest battles in the time it takes to finish a commute, while learning interesting facts long forgotten or never known.

World War II was fought on a scale unlike anything before or since in human history, and the unfathomable casualty counts are attributable in large measure to the carnage inflicted between Nazi Germany and the Soviet Union during Hitler's invasion of Russia and Stalin's desperate defense. The invasion came in 1941 following a nonaggression pact signed between the two in 1939, which allowed Hitler to focus his attention on the west without having to worry about an attack from the eastern front. While Germany was focusing on the west, the Soviet Union sent large contingents of troops to the border region between the two countries, and Stalin's plan to take territory in Poland and the Baltic States angered Hitler. By 1940, Hitler viewed Stalin as a major threat and had made the decision to invade Russia: "In the course of this contest, Russia must be disposed of...Spring 1941. The quicker we smash Russia the better." (Hoyt, p. 17)

The surprise achieved by the German invasion in 1941 allowed their armies to advance rapidly across an incredibly wide front, but once winter set in, the two sides had to dig in and brace for German sieges of Russian cities.

While a legend exists today that Hitler's strategic fecklessness destroyed Germany's chances, despite the wise objections of the Wehrmacht general staff (OKW), the actual situation in 1941 resembled the precise reverse of this familiar historical trope. The historian Robert Forczyk argues convincingly that the Fuhrer retained his full strategic acumen in 1941, until he ill-advisedly adopted the suggestions of the OKW and diverted forces in a winter campaign to seize the Soviet capital, leading to the Battle of Moscow (Forczyk I, 2006, 8-9).

The Third Reich's dictator initially viewed Moscow as a relatively trivial objective, only to be seized once the Red Army suffered defeat in detail. In fact, he planned a pause during the bitter Russian winter, conserving German strength for a fresh offensive in spring of 1942. Wisely, According to Chief of Operations Colonel Heusinger, Hitler manifested "an instinctive aversion to treading the same path as Napoleon [...] Moscow gives him a sinister feeling."

Despite the obstructionism of the OKW General Staff - centered around Fedor von Bock, Franz Halder and Brauschitsch, who obsessed over taking Moscow and reacted to the Fuhrer's focus on the south with open rage and contempt – the southern offensive went ahead, securing another stunning victory over the Soviets and seizing the economically vital Donets Basin. In the meantime, Stalin immolated hundreds of thousands of his own soldiers in futile attacks against Army Group Center, holding the German front facing Moscow.

Halder ultimately drafted the plan for Operation Typhoon, the October 1941 thrust towards Moscow, and Hitler showed considerable reluctance to agree to the attack, believing it best if the Germans suspended operations until spring. Halder and his OKW clique persisted, however, badgering the Fuhrer until Hitler imprudently yielded to their demands. The head of the Third Reich apparently succumbed to Halder's and Bock's importuning mostly due to unrestrained ebullience over the southern success. He felt that at this stage, "nothing could go wrong." In doing so, he forgot the keenly insightful precept of the 17th century samurai general Oda

Nobunaga, who declared, "After a victory, tighten your helmet straps." Far from maintaining his focus, however, Hitler relaxed and let his guard down. His surrender to Halder's impractical plan signaled the beginning of an ominous reversal of Wehrmacht fortunes whose seeds sprouted at the Battle of Moscow.

The Greatest Battles in History: The Battle of Moscow During World War II chronicles the operations that saw the Soviets push back the Nazis from their capital. Along with pictures of important people, places, and events, you will learn about the Battle of Moscow like never before.

The Greatest Battles in History: The Battle of Moscow During World War II

About Charles River Editors

Introduction

   Chapter 1: The Nonaggression Pact and Operation Barbarossa

   Chapter 2: The Beginning of Operation Typhoon

   Chapter 3: Trapping the Soviets

   Chapter 4: The Fall of the Hexenkessel

   Chapter 5: The Drive to Kalinin

   Chapter 6: The Final Phases of the Battle for Moscow

   Online Resources

   Bibliography

Chapter 1: The Nonaggression Pact and Operation Barbarossa

"History shows that there are no invincible armies and that there never have been." – Joseph Stalin

Although Soviet premier Joseph Stalin was worried about internal enemies throughout the 1930s, the rest of Europe was preoccupied with the Spanish Civil War and the rise to power of Adolf Hitler and the Nazis in Germany. Seeing this as both an opportunity and a threat, Stalin threw the support of Soviet Russia behind the Popular Front supporting the Spanish Republican government in the Civil War. Not only did he send tanks and aircraft to Spain, but he also sent about 850 personnel to man them and advise the rebels in their fight.

Stalin

However, Stalin's main concern, like that of the rest of the world at that time, was Germany. Although the Treaty of Versailles that ended World War I had placed limits on German rearmament, those provisions were routinely being ignored by the Germans, and European powers thus sensed their own rearmament was a priority. Concerned that Hitler would soon turn his sights on Russia, Stalin began to put out feelers among other European countries about forming an alliance, but initially, his offer was met with skepticism. English Prime Minister Neville Chamberlain disliked Stalin and would have nothing to do with his offers. On the other hand, Winston Churchill, who at the time was trying to rally his countrymen to the threat posed by Hitler, saw the practical benefits of the alliance Stalin was offering, saying in a speech on May 4, 1938: "There is no means of maintaining an eastern front against Nazi aggression without the active aid of Russia. Russian interests are deeply concerned in preventing Herr Hitler's designs on Eastern Europe. It should still be possible to range all the States and peoples from the Baltic to the Black Sea in one solid front against a new outrage of invasion. Such a front, if established in good heart, and with resolute and efficient military arrangements, combined with the strength of the Western Powers, may yet confront Hitler, Goering, Himmler, Ribbentrop, Goebbels and co. with forces the German people would be reluctant to challenge."

Churchill

Hitler

On September 30 1938, Prime Minister Neville Chamberlain returned to Britain and promised the British "peace for our time", waving a copy of the agreement he had signed with Adolf Hitler and Benito Mussolini in Munich the day before. Of course, Chamberlain and Munich have become synonymous with appeasement, a word that has since taken on very negative connotations, and war would explode across the continent exactly 11 months later.

Chamberlain holds up the Munich Agreement

When Chamberlain visited Hitler in September, Stalin became convinced that England was planning a secret pact with Germany against the Soviet Union, so he decided to try to beat them to the punch. Stalin contacted Hitler and proposed that they form an alliance, going as far as to fire his Commissar of Foreign Affairs, Maxim Litinov, a Jew who was an unacceptable ambassador to Hitler's government. Litinov's replacement met the following month with German foreign minister Joachim von Ribbentrop, and on August 28, 1939, they signed the Nazi-Soviet Pact, in which both sides promised to remain neutral in any future war.

From 1936-1939, Hitler took a series of steps in further violation of the Treaty of Versailles, but Europe still refused to confront him. The "appeasement" of Hitler by France and Great Britain before World War II is now roundly condemned, a fact Chamberlain himself came to understand in 1939: "Everything that I have worked for, everything that I have believed in during my public life, has crashed into ruins."

On September 1, 1939, the world was changed forever. Despite several attempts by the French and British to appease Hitler's Nazi regime and avoid war, most notably allowing Hitler to annex the Sudetenland, Germany invaded Poland on that day, officially starting the deadliest conflict in human history. For the French and British, the Nazi invasion of Poland promised war, and by September 3, both countries declared war on Germany. Meanwhile, the Soviet Union, fresh off signing a nonaggression pact with Hitler, invaded the Baltic. France and the United Kingdom, treating the Soviet attack on Finland as tantamount to entering the war on the side of the Germans, responded to the Soviet invasion by supporting the expulsion of the Soviets from the

League of Nations.

Though Germany and Russia had promised each other neutrality, Stalin had no delusions that they were friends. Instead, he used this time to build up his forces for what he saw as an inevitable invasion. First, on the heels of the German invasion of Poland in September 1939, Stalin had his troops invade and reclaim the land Russia had lost in World War I. He then turned his attention to Finland, which was only 100 miles from the newly named Leningrad. He initially tried to negotiate with the Finnish government for some sort of treaty of mutual support, but when that failed, he simply invaded. While the giant Russian army ultimately won, the fact that little Finland held them off for three months demonstrated how poorly organized the bigger force was.

Britain and France also began a naval blockade of Germany on September 3 which aimed to damage the country's economy and war effort, but the Nazis would blitzkrieg across the continent over the next year and eventually overwhelm France in mid-1940, leaving the British to fight alone. For the first two years of the war, it looked as though the Axis powers may very well win the war and usher in a new world order.

Initially, Stalin believed he had several years to build up his army before Germany could possibly invade Russia, figuring it would at least take the Germans that long to conquer France and Britain. However, when France fell quickly in 1940, it seemed he might have miscalculated, so he again sent Molotov to Berlin to stall for time. Meanwhile, Hitler trained his sights on Britain, turning his attention to destroying the Royal Air Force as a pre-requisite for the invasion of Britain. Given how quickly the Nazis had experienced success during the war thus far, perhaps the Luftwaffe's notorious leader, Hermann Goering, was not being entirely unrealistic in 1940 when he boasted, "My Luftwaffe is invincible...And so now we turn to England. How long will this one last - two, three weeks?"

Goering

Goering, of course, was proven wrong. During the desperate air battles that ensued, Britain's investment in radar and modern fighters, coupled with a German switch in tactics, won the day. The Battle of Britain was the only battle of the war fought entirely by air, as the Luftwaffe battled the British Royal Air Force for months during the second half of 1940 and early 1941. The Luftwaffe also bombed British infrastructure and indiscriminately bombed civilian targets, but Germany's attempt to overwhelm the British was repulsed by the Royal Air Force. British cities were targeted, and Churchill's very public tours of wreckage helped make him an icon symbolizing the determined, stubborn resistance of the nation. This was the first real check to Nazi expansion, and as only Churchill could put it, "Their generals told their Prime Minister and his divided Cabinet, 'In three weeks England will have her neck wrung like a chicken.' Some chicken! Some neck!"

In March 1941, Germany invaded Greece and Yugoslavia in an effort to shore up its right flank prior to attacking Russia. Stalin knew that if he could delay a German invasion through the summer of 1941, Russia would be safe for another year, but unfortunately for the Soviets, Molotov's mission failed and Hitler began to earnestly plan the invasion of Russia by the end of Spring 1941. From the German point of view, although Hitler strongly wished to attack the Soviet Union, his generals were almost all against such a course of action. As Field Marshal Paul von Kleist wrote, "We did not underrate the Red Army as it is commonly imagined. The last Germany military attaché in Moscow, General Ernst Koestring - a very able man - had kept us well informed about the state of the Russian army. But Hitler refused to credit that information." (Hoyt, p. 24)

At the same time, Hitler tried to convince his military command that the Russians were making preparations to attack the Germans, but again, his generals seemed to be unconvinced of this. As Field Marshal Gerd von Rundstedt explained, "In the first place the Russians seemed to be taken by surprise when we crossed the frontier. On my front we saw no signs of offensive preparations in the forward zone, though there were some farther back. They had twenty-five divisions in the Carpathian sector, facing the Hungarian frontier, and I had expected they would swing around and strike at my right flank as it advanced. Instead they retreated. I deduced from this that they were not in a state of readiness for offensive operations, and hence that the Russian command had not been intending to launch an offensive at an early date." (Hoyt, p. 24)

Despite the military's doubts, it was Hitler making the call, and since military secrets are typically the hardest to keep, Stalin soon began to hear rumors of the invasion. However, when Churchill contacted him in April 1941 warning him that German troops seemed to be massing on Russia's border, Stalin remained dubious. Stalin felt even more secure in his position when the Germans failed to invade that May, but what he did not realize was that Hitler had simply overstretched German forces in Yugoslavia and only planned to delay the invasion by a few weeks. Hitler aimed to destroy Stalin's Communist regime, but he also hoped to gain access to resources in Russia, particularly oil. Thus, throughout the first half of 1941, Germany dug in to safeguard against an Allied invasion of Western Europe and began to mobilize millions of troops to invade the Soviet Union. Stalin even refused to believe the report of a German defector who claimed that the troops were massing on the Soviet border at that very moment.

All the way up until the launch of Operation Barbarossa, Stalin believed Hitler would not attack in 1941, and as the Soviet media reported just days before the German invasion began, "Despite the obvious absurdity of rumors about a forthcoming war, responsible circles in Moscow have authorized a statement that according to evidence in the possession of the Soviet Union both Germany and the Soviet Union are fulfilling to the letter the terms of the Soviet Nonaggression Pact. Germany troop movements in the eastern and northern parts of Germany are explained by other motives that have no connection with Soviet-German relations. It is false to state that the Soviet Union is preparing for a war with Germany." (Hoyt, p. 18)

On June 22, 1941, Stalin had to admit he was wrong, because 3,400 German tanks and 3 million German soldiers rolled across the Russian border, beginning the deadliest campaigns of World War II. Hitler boasted, "before three months have passed, we shall witness a collapse of Russia, the like of which has never been seen in history." Not surprisingly, Soviet propaganda ensured citizens that the Germans would be beaten back, with Molotov informing them, "Citizens and Citizenesses of the Soviet Union! Today, at four o'clock in the morning, without addressing any grievances to the Soviet Union, without declaration of war, German forces fell on our country, attacked our frontiers in many places and bombed our cities...an act of treachery unprecedented in the history of civilized nations...The Red Army and the whole nation will wage a victorious Patriotic War for our beloved country, for honour, for liberty...Our cause is just. The enemy will be beaten. Victory will be ours."

However, when the German offensive began, Soviet units were unprepared to meet the invasion, and their lack of preparedness meant that by the time Soviet leaders at the Kremlin announced that the country was now at war, German troops and armored divisions had already made their way deep into Russian territory. Adding to the problems among Soviet troops was Stalin's complete lack of competent officers, which was a direct effect of his purges of the military in 1937 and 1938. Conspicuous among the Russian officers purged by Stalin was Marshal Mikhail Tukhachevsky, deputy commissar of defense, who had been actively attempting to modernize the Soviet army at the time he was convicted and shot.

The Soviet purges meant not only that the army had lost its best commanders but also that Soviet officers in 1941 were constantly afraid for their lives, which precluded them from taking the initiative in the field and ensured they strictly followed directives from the Kremlin. Therefore, when Stalin took command over the newly created State Defense Committee to oversee the Soviet war effort, his lack of military skill was compounded by the lack of intelligent officers on whose advice he might have been able to draw, as well as the army's willingness to follow his orders without question, even when those orders cost thousands of Russian lives.

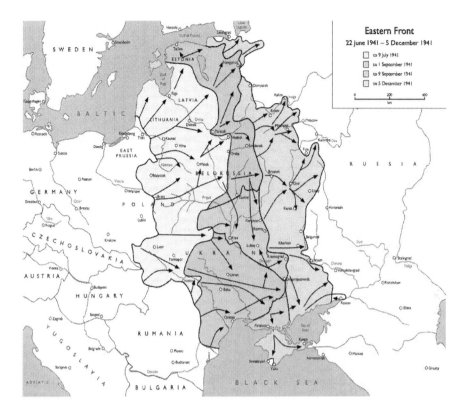

A map of Germany's progress during the offensive in 1941

Chapter 2: The Beginning of Operation Typhoon

The genesis of Operation Typhoon lay in Fuhrer Directive 35, which did not actually call directly for taking Moscow. This Directive, again showing more strategic sanity than generally credited to Hitler, ordered "a decisive operation against Army Group Timoshenko, which is conducting unsuccessful offensive operations on Army Group Centre's front. It must be destroyed decisively before the onset of winter. […] after destroying the main mass of Timoshenko's group of forces […] Army Group Centre is to begin pursuing enemy forces along the Moscow axis." (Forczyk I, 2006, 12).

The OKW, cooperating with Field Marshal Fedor von Bock, the commander of Army Group Center, interpreted this directive very generously as they prepared plans in August and early September. In keeping with their fixation on Moscow, these men made the Soviet capital their main objective, as opposed to merely pounding Russian general Semyon Timoshenko's armies into submission. They code-named the scheme "Operation Typhoon."

Bock

Timoshenko

The German lines of supply experienced numerous problems in Russia – though the Soviet forces suffered even greater logistical headaches much of the time, in part due to the paranoid irrationality of Soviet totalitarian government – and relied heavily on truck transport. Hitler ordered no less than 3,500 new trucks sent to Army Group Center during the preparations for Operation Typhoon to carry gasoline, supplies, and ammunition. Moreover, 307 additional tanks also reached the Eastern Front for Operation Typhoon, of which 50 were Panzer IV medium tanks, 166 were Panzer III medium tanks (already undergunned for the era), and the balance Czech-based Pz-38(t) light tanks (Forczyk II, 2013, 116). In all, the Wehrmacht mustered 70 divisions for the Operation; 47 infantry divisions comprised the bulk of Army Group Center, but 15 Panzer divisions (mustering at least 1,000 tanks) and 8 motorized infantry divisions gave the expedition both mobility and teeth. The Germans organized these divisions into six armies.

Soviet forces found themselves outnumbered by anywhere from 1.5:1 to 2:1 in personnel and various kinds of equipment, but with Moscow at their backs, the men facing the Wehrmacht killing machine exhibited fanatical courage and determination. The waning year also strictly limited the operational days before foul weather set in. Approximately 894,000 Soviet soldiers formed three fronts facing Army Group Center. These men, deployed in an amateurish manner by their inexperienced commanders, benefited from the support of 849 tanks, consisting of 47 KV-1 heavy tanks, 94 T-34 medium tanks, and hundreds of largely obsolete light tanks. These ragged, exhausted men, with little ammunition and few supplies, found themselves concentrated close to the front due to grandiose Stalinist plans for an offensive.

Soviet T-26 light tanks at the battle

A Soviet T-34 tank during the fighting

Lieutenant General Ivan Konev commanded the main portion of the front, with six armies at his disposal. Commanding the reserve force of six armies behind him, Semyon Budyonny remained convinced of the superiority of horsed cavalry to tanks – and, indeed, of lances to rifles. "Pulya dura, shtyk molodyets," his favorite aphorism derived from Suvorov, translates as "the bullet is a fool, the lance is a stout fellow," and Budyonny proved grimly faithful to it by viciously participating in the judicial murder of Mikhail Tukhachevksy, the modernizer of Soviet tank warfare. The sly survivor Andrei Yeremenko, meanwhile, commanded four armies on the Bryansk Front, guarding Moscow's southern flank.

Konev

Budyonny

Russian cavalry at Moscow

During the operations, the Panzer III and Panzer IV tanks proved inferior to the Russians' T-34 and KV-1 tanks, but German tactics more than evened the balance. Heinz Guderian noted that during the Third Reich's and Soviet Union's brief alliance, questions by visiting Soviet military men made him suspect that the Soviets might have superior tank designs: "The Russian officers in question firmly refused to believe that the Panzer IV was in fact our heaviest tank. They said repeatedly that we must be hiding our newest models from them, and complained that we were not carrying out Hitler's order to show them everything. The military commission was so insistent on this point that eventually our manufacturers and Ordnance Office officials concluded: 'It seems that the Russians must already possess better and heavier tanks than we do.'" (Guderian, 1964, 84).

The Germans' tanks did not lack its own advantages, however. Every German tank included a powerful radio, while only 1 in 10 Russian tanks possessed a radio, usually with a very short range and weak signal. The panzers operated as part of a sophisticated radio net, connected to all levels of command, making precise coordination possible and providing invaluable real-time information to the panzer commanders.

The inexperienced Russian crews also fought fully "buttoned up," depriving their commander of clear vision of the situation. Worse, they often neglected to turn on the tank's ventilation system, resulting in violently sick or fully incapacitated crews from ammonia fumes. Soviet commanders also frequently committed tanks in small groups, squandering their effectiveness, though some showed tactical acumen equal to any panzer commander of the Third Reich.

The Germans originally planned to launch Operation Typhoon in mid-September, giving themselves two additional weeks prior to winter's arrival to execute their design, but delays set in, however. Army Group Center lay at the end of extremely long overland supply lines, and due to lack of rail transport in many locations, panzers had to drive up to 600 miles under their own power while mustering for the offensive. After traveling so far over Russia's appallingly bad roads, the Germans spent considerable time repairing and overhauling the battered vehicles.

A picture of a vehicle stuck in mud on a road outside Moscow

While the Germans prepared, the Soviets dug in, even though the Russians believed the Germans would mount their next offensive in the south to pierce even deeper into the Soviet Union's underbelly. Heinrich Haape reported, "East of the Mezha, the Russians prepared a strong system of trenches, bunkers, tank-traps and barbed-wire entanglements. They laid minefields, reinforced their front-line troops, brought up supplies and gathered their strength to stand against us once more. We had to sit helplessly … and listen to stories brought back by our patrols of the rapidly developing Russian defensive system." (Stahel I, 2013, 55).

Guderian opened operations on September 30th, but the Soviets initially mistook his thrust for a feint since the majority of Army Group Center remained immobile. Thus, the Battle of Moscow began fully at dawn on October 2nd, 1941, in approved Wehrmacht style; a huge artillery bombardment swept over the Soviet positions at 5:30 a.m. sharp, pulverizing and stunning the frontline defenders. Luftwaffe bombers followed the rolling curtain of artillery fire, dropping their lethal payloads on the Russian soldiers, after which panzers rumbled forward through the gray predawn gloom, the armored spearhead followed by swarms of experienced, highly trained Wehrmacht infantry.

Guderian

The tanks achieved dramatic breakthroughs, commanded by such armored warfare luminaries as Heinz Guderian (leading Panzer Group 2), Hermann Hoth (in charge of Panzer Group 3), and Erich Hoepner (Panzer Group 4's talented leader, destined to end his life slowly strangling in a piano wire noose after the July 20th, 1944 bomb plot against Hitler). With dry conditions under a clear sky and bright sun, the panzers traversed the Russian roads up to 12 miles on the first day, and since the Soviets only had light tanks with green crews, the German armored forces scarcely believed their good fortune.

Hoepner

Hoth

A picture of German panzers at the battle

General Erhard Raus' 6th Panzer Division, forming the leading unit of Hoth's Panzer Group 3, pierced even deeper into Soviet territory. The division reached the upper Dnieper 18 miles from the starting point on the first day and, critically, took two good bridges intact. This had the effect of both securing Hoth's line of advance and denying the Russians in the sector any easy retreat past the river. Nevertheless, the Soviets attempted a withdrawal that night, as Raus reported: "That night I ordered the renewed employment, by the entire division, of the defensive hedgehog tactics that *Kampfgruppe* Raus had routinely utilized in its drive through the Baltic countries. […] Enemy troop units were moving all around the entire system of panzer hedgehogs as soon as darkness fell."

Raus

Meanwhile, the German infantry encountered stiffer resistance. Though badly mauled by artillery, bombing, and tank attacks, the Soviet infantry rallied bravely and fought hard to hold their remaining positions. Here and there the Germans suffered notable casualties, but eventually, the Soviet infantry succumbed, and the penetration broadened and strengthened. During the advance, the German infantry frequently found large piles of Soviet soldiers already killed in passing by tank machine guns. One particular item of note in the first days of the offensive consisted of wrecked American-made Jeeps, whose strange appearance drew the curiosity of the Wehrmacht soldiers (Seaton, 1993, 76-77). These vehicles marked the first trickles of Lend-Lease, destined to grow into a flood that kept the Soviet Union in the war.

October 3rd witnessed even more successes for the Germans, while the situation rapidly worsened for the Soviets. Arthur Wollschlaeger led four panzers into the city of Orel and captured it with its strategically vital bridges and railroad yards intact. As his tiny force seized the city of 140,000 inhabitants, Wollschlaeger noted, "City life was still in full swing. When the citizens of Orel saw us, they fled into the buildings and side streets, white as ghosts." Wollschlaeger's men represented the very tip of Guderian's Panzer Group 2, while Guderian's men encountered and routed a rifle battalion consisting of Russian women near Orel on the same day, another strange sight for the all-male Wehrmacht. Other units found the machinery of disassembled factories stacked in the railyards, ready for shipment eastward but now unexpectedly overtaken by the German advance (Seaton, 1993, 77).

With the skies still clear, the roads firm and dry, and the Luftwaffe providing close air support when needed, Hoth and Hoepner's Panzer Groups each pushed 30 miles past the starting point. Both Ivan Konev and Andrei Yeremenko requested Stalin's permission to fall back, fearing another vast encirclement such as those which already yielded 3 million prisoners to the Germans during the previous three months, but the Soviet dictator curtly refused. Understandably fearing summary execution or torture in NKVD cells followed by a show trial and execution, the Red Army commanders held their ground as the tide of German armor and infantry penetrated deep into their rear. A Soviet commander attempted to attack the flank of Raus' 6th Panzer Division on the 3rd near Kholm in order to stop or delay the advance of Hermann Hoth's Panzer Group 3. 100 Soviet tanks took part, but they attempted the attack through thickly wooded terrain, which dispersed them into small, uncoordinated groups. The Germans quickly deployed PaK anti-tank guns and 88mm Flak guns and shot the attack to pieces, claiming 80 kills in a matter of hours and forcing the remaining Soviet armor to retreat.

The Wehrmacht and the German population showed the same incredulous reaction to the fresh advance despite its initial successes. Nobody understood why the war continued following the massive defeats inflicted on the Soviet Union, but Stalin's ideological intransigence and the Russians' clear awareness that Hitler intended their literal extermination as subhumans obviously gave the Soviets plenty of motive to keep fighting. Of course, that determination was less clear to those who were constantly being given Goebbels' propaganda, and Hitler addressed his people in Berlin, reiterating that the fresh offensive would smash the Soviet army and end the threat of communism forever.

Though the ground attack moved forward initially with the inexorability of a juggernaut, the Luftwaffe failed to master the skies over the region near Moscow. Spread thin over a huge space, the German pilots fought with skill and professionalism but found the Soviet air forces much superior to the barely-trained draftees dying in hordes on the ground. On October 5th, Heinz Guderian himself narrowly avoided death when Soviet bombers attacked his airfield headquarters at Sevsk, destroying some German planes on the runway and shattering the windows of the room where Guderian and his staff stood conferring.

A picture of Soviet planes near Nazi positions around Moscow

Picture of a downed German plane being shown off in Moscow

Chapter 3: Trapping the Soviets

During October 3rd and 4th, the Panzer Groups attacked and maneuvered to trap entire Soviet armies in "pockets" – in the vivid German terminology "Hexenkessel" or "witches' cauldrons" – where surrender would quickly follow. In the south, Guderian's panzers sought to create a pocket around Bryansk, while Vyazma formed the center of another encirclement made by the planned juncture of Hoth's and Hoepner's Panzer Groups. Luftflotte 2 of the Luftwaffe supported the panzer thrusts constantly, directing devastating Stuka dive-bomber airstrikes anywhere that Soviet infantry or armor concentrated in an effort to resist the offensive.

Konev, understanding all too well the fate awaiting his armies if the double envelopment closed its jaws around them, launched multiple counterattacks in addition to the ill-fated tank attack near Kholm on October 3rd. The fighting continued for three days, through October 5th, during which the Germans destroyed dozens of Soviet tanks but lost significant (albeit lesser) numbers of their own.

Despite the Soviet attempts, the encirclement annihilated the Soviet 43rd Army and trapped the 20th and 24th Armies within a hostile girdle of Wehrmacht men and steel. The commanders at the OKH headquarters, visited by Hitler himself on October 4th, showed great energy and verve, expecting another stunning victory, and the Fuhrer spoke airily of Guderian driving through to Tula and then Moscow. However, the inexorable specter of supply failures began to manifest itself almost simultaneously with his visit, the first sign that the Wehrmacht simply lacked the means to carry out Operation Typhoon as planned. Guderian called for 500 cubic meters of gasoline but received only 20% of that on October 6th, seriously slowing his advance, and a chorus of similar requests came in from Hoth, Hoepner, and their subordinates as their efforts to maneuver began faltering even before completing the Bryansk and Vyazma encirclements. Exacerbating the problem, the Germans' tanks all featured gasoline engines due to procrastination by Hitler's engineers, while the Soviets' diesel tank engines needed far less fuel by volume to continue operating. The Panzer I tank included a diesel engine, but its obsolescence prevented its fielding on the eastern front, at least in a mainline combat role.

As the Germans slowed, the Soviets stepped up their counterattacks. T-34 tanks delivered a startling reverse to the 4th Panzer Division, part of Heinz Guderian's Panzer Group 2, near Mtsensk on October 6th. The German defeat came despite their superior numbers, with 56 panzer III and IV tanks facing off against 45 T-34s and other Soviet tanks. The 4th Panzer Division commander, Langermann-Erlencamp, repeatedly attacked on October 7th, 8th, and 9th, but the Soviet commander, Mikhail Katukov, skillfully used flanking attacks to destroy most of the Division's panzers and held on to Mtsensk, halting a small but significant part of the Operation Typhoon advance in its tracks.

Katukov

On October 5th, at around noon, Stalin finally realized the folly of his orders for Konev and Yeremenko to hold their ground. The crucial moment arrived when scouting aircraft found an unopposed column of German armor and infantry, 12 miles in length, approaching Yukhnov with no Soviet forces between it and Moscow, 114 miles distant. The Soviet dictator ordered a new defense line called the Mozhaysk Defense Line between the column and Moscow, while giving Konev and Yeremenko full authorization to retreat.

As the Soviets finally changed plans, the Germans struggled to close the encirclement during the end of the first week in October and into the start of the second week. Fedor von Bock feuded savagely with several of his subordinates, causing further delays, but even still, nearly 79,000 prisoners fell into German hands even before the Vyazma Pocket's closure, along with hundreds of tanks, artillery pieces, soft-skinned vehicles, and aircraft, signaling yet another crushing defeat for the Red Army.

Facing disaster, Stalin recalled Marshal Georgy Zhukov from Leningrad on October 7th and sent him to review the situation. Zhukov managed to convince Stalin not to execute Konev by asking for the disgraced general to be made his second in command – Konev's predicament, after all, was completely the result of Stalin's own incompetent orders – and quickly realized that the dictator had doomed his own armies by refusing earlier permission to retreat. Zhukov even dared to praise Konev's performance: "Shooting Koniev will not improve anything or encourage anyone. It will only produce a bad impression in the army. Shooting Pavlov was no use at all. Everyone knew that Pavlov should never have been put in charge of anything larger than a division … But Koniev is not Pavlov – he is an intelligent man. He can still be serviceable."

Zhukov

Stalin inquired belligerently whether Zhukov counted Konev as a personal friend, but the Soviet commander remained adamant and Stalin eventually backed down. Some accounts suggest he threatened to kill both men if Moscow fell, but regardless of these possible threats, Zhukov focused on building the Mozhaysk Defense Line after his elevation to command in place of Konev on October 10th. He did little to relieve the men trapped in either hexenkessel, appearing to view them as a sunk cost, but he appreciated the time their sacrifice bought him. Though his staff discussed airdropping food, fuel, ammunition, and medicine, no flights ever took place for that purpose.

Despite supply difficulties and desperately brave Soviet resistance, the hard-charging Heinz Guderian completed the Bryansk encirclement by October 6th, trapping the Soviet 3rd, 14th, and 50th Armies. Yeremenko attempted to coordinate the efforts of the armies under his command, but he gradually lost radio contact with the units comprising them, and radio communications with Moscow failed also. Yeremenko, despite his deep fear of Stalin's wrath, ordered his men to break out and escape much sooner than Konev did to the north, recognizing the hopelessness of the situation and choosing to possibly incur the Soviet dictator's wrath by disobeying his foolish orders.

Picture of a Soviet radio operator during the battle

As a result, the Germans completed the two enormous encirclements successfully even while suffering fuel shortages and considerable casualties due to dogged Soviet counterattacks. The Soviets continued fighting despite their encirclement, forcing the Wehrmacht to commit 28 divisions to their destruction and greatly weakening the thrust towards Moscow. Ultimately, 514,000 Soviet prisoners fell into the Third Reich's hands, the largest single surrender of Operation Barbarossa to date.

Though Stalin had thrown away another eight armies through his strategic blundering, the weather abruptly changed and did more to impede the Germans than the Red Army. Heavy rain fell on October 6th and 7th, immediately crippling the Wehrmacht's mobility, and tanks and other vehicles used extra portions of already scarce fuel fighting their way laboriously through the muck. Fleeing Soviet journalist Vasily Grossman gloated, "There's rain, snow, hailstones, a liquid, bottomless swamp, black pastry mixed by thousands and thousands of boots, wheels, caterpillars. And everyone is happy once again. The Germans must get stuck in our hellish autumn." (Stahel I, 2013, 81).

Guderian's encirclement at Bryansk proved relatively porous due to his lack of manpower, while the Vyazma "hexenkessel" showed considerably greater security. Nevertheless, large numbers of Red Army soldiers escaped eastward, even as the majority died or surrendered in the two pockets. The Germans reduced the Vyazma pocket systematically on October 8th and 9th with merciless artillery and bombing attacks, combined with massive infantry advances. General Erhard Raus vividly described some of the action during the closing of the Vyazma pocket on October 9th, when he said that the 6th and 7th Panzer Divisions, working together, "resembled a mighty battleship, smashing all targets within reach with the heavy caliber of its broadsides. Artillery and mortar shells from 300 throats of fire hailed down on the Soviet batteries and tanks. Soon the Russian tanks were in flames, the batteries transformed into smoking heaps of rubble, and the lines of skirmishers swept away by a swath of fire from hundreds of machine guns."

Also on October 9th, Hans von Greiffenberg, in command of the Vyazma pocket forces, ordered the encircled Soviets eliminated with extreme vigor. He gave a simple directive: "All corps have the order: 'Forwards, forwards, forwards!'" The Soviet 19th Army attempted to break out of the encirclement on October 10th, supported by other units, but Hoepner's Panzer Group 4 and the 23rd Infantry Division under Major General Heinz Hellmich fought this breakout attempt and eventually pushed it back. That said, the 19th Army's effort to extricate itself cost Hoepner's and Hellmich's men dearly thanks to the intense fighting, and the Germans noted with dismay that the Russians fought with great tenacity, with 5 men dying for every 1 who surrendered. This was the case even though appallingly bad Soviet logistics meant that at least half of the Red Army soldiers carried no weapons at all; they simply followed the armed men so that when these died, they could arm themselves with the fallen man's rifle. Not surprisingly, the Wehrmacht soldiers could hardly believe what they were seeing.

Chapter 4: The Fall of the Hexenkessel

The drive on Moscow slowed and stuttered to a near halt as the weather continued worsening. Though the panzers negotiated the mud with considerable difficulty, the wheeled trucks and horse-drawn supply wagons bringing them gasoline could not maneuver at all. German engineers struggled to "corduroy" the roads with logs, but the process remained time consuming and the bumpy drive damaged the worn, overused trucks further. General Raus noted that most of the tanks had now been driven continuously for 6,000-7,000 miles, and that in the absence of spare parts, the men kept them running by cannibalizing other tanks. This, of course, reduced the number of working vehicles as effectively as combat losses, though the general noted forlornly that the hulls might be salvageable for eventual remanufacture.

As heavy snow fell on October 9th and 10th, the Germans contrived to force an advance despite the staggering obstacles. Junkers Ju-52 aircraft airlifted several hundred tons of fuel daily to the advance units, enough to permit a laborious forward movement, and some commanders pressed their SdKfz 251 Hanomag halftracks into service as improvised fuel trucks, gaining a little mobility at the cost of depriving their infantry of the protection of these early armored personnel carriers.

Meanwhile, on October 10th and 11th, the Soviets continued their frantic efforts to break out of the "pockets." Frequently, single companies of German motorized infantry blocked the path of division-sized Russian units, and in some cases, these small forces found themselves under constant attack for 24 continuous hours. Mikhail Lukin, commander of the Soviet 19th Army, did his utmost to organize the men for a successful breakout. The Red Army soldiers siphoned the gasoline out of their wheeled vehicles, such as trucks and command cars, and used it to fill the engines of tanks and artillery tractors, deemed to be the highest value assets still in the encircled forces' protection. The Soviet artillery fired off all their remaining shells at pre-designated targets such as railyards and then destroyed their guns to keep them out of German hands.

The attack aimed for the village of Bogoroditskoye, across the Bobria River and through low-lying swampy ground that the Soviet soldiers soon dubbed "the Valley of Death." At the last minute, Lukin found it necessary to deal with the anxieties of an important subordinate: "At this moment, General V.P. Vashkevich, upon whom I was placing all hopes, raised objections regarding the timing of the attack and the haste with which the divisions were being committed into battle, so again I had to try to convince him […] that if we didn't break out that night, next day the enemy would crush us […] We said our farewells, shook hands, and he left."

Vast numbers of Soviet soldiers died as they attempted to push through the German defenses over open ground. Machine guns raked the crowd, rifle fire picked off single men, and artillery, mortars, and direct fire from the deadly 88mm anti-aircraft guns shredded human flesh and vehicular steel with impartial brutality. Some men managed to break out eastward, and those who did so at night frequently escaped, but during the day, mobile panzer units relentlessly hunted and slaughtered fleeing soldiers who managed to survive the lethal cordon surrounding the pockets. Still, the sheer desperation of the Soviets to escape made a lingering impression on their tormenters. The 11th Panzer Division officer Walter Shaefer-Kehnert described the surreal vision of a Soviet breakout attempt: "I saw one of these attacks coming early in the morning. We were sitting on the top of the hills, there was fog going down to the river valley, and when the fog came up it was like a herd of vehicles and men coming up by the thousand and it made your blood freeze."

Most of the men trying to escape ended up as prisoners or as jumbled, shattered corpses freezing in the churned mud. The 111th Panzer Grenadier Regiment alone took 3,000 prisoners and killed 2,000 more men in the course of two days, sustaining considerable losses in killed and wounded in the process. In the meantime, von Greiffenberg's soldiers pressed into the Vyazma pocket from the west, squeezing the remaining Soviets into a smaller and smaller area. Vast columns of hundreds of thousands of prisoners stumbled westward through the deep, clinging mud of the roads, including Lukin himself. His staff eventually abandoned him in a peasant hut after a bad leg wound rendered him practically immobile. The Germans took him prisoner, eventually amputated his leg when they could not save it, and attempted to recruit him for the Wehrmacht, an effort which ultimately failed.

Many of the men taken prisoner died in any case, often in a far more lingering and excruciating manner than those cut down by machine gun fire and high explosive shells. Some German guards reported starving soldiers literally tearing one or two of their comrades to pieces daily and devouring them in desperation. At one location in Poland, the Germans penned 100,000 luckless Soviets in the open inside a huge barbed wire entanglement and simply guarded them until every single one starved to death, while shooting any who attempted to escape.

Though some Germans felt pity for the Russians taken prisoner and then murdered by inches in this fashion, other exhibited savage indifference or hatred, showing how completely totalitarian propaganda could transform otherwise ordinary men into hardened killers. Maximilian Siry, a German officer, felt that the Wehrmacht's defeat stemmed from their excessively lenient and gentle treatment of prisoners: "One mustn't admit it openly, but we were far too soft. All these horrors have landed us in the soup now. But if we'd carried them through to the hilt, made the people disappear completely – no one would say a thing. These half measures are always wrong. […] We've seen that we cannot conduct a war because we're not hard enough, not barbaric enough." (Stahel II, 2015, 44-45).

Vashkevich, on the other hand, was one of the few who successfully broke out that day. He gathered portions of the 1282nd and 1286th Rifle Regiments 12 miles away from the breakout point, along with some artillery units and naval infantry. The men slept while Vashkevich and his officers kept watch for other escapees throughout the day, but only a bare handful joined them. As the sound of firing died away, Vashkevich realized that the bulk of the 19th Army remained trapped or had perished, so he led his men eastward.

The 20th and 24th Soviet Armies, also penned in by the Vyazma encirclement, attempted to break out as well. Most Russian records of these two armies remain classified even as of the early 21st century, but a few radio messages reproduced in various official records indicate the same mix of desperate courage and chaos as was the case with the 19th Army. One radio operator reported no less than three generals dying while leading a single vain effort to burst through the German lines on October 13th.

By the morning of the 14th, the 20th and 24th Armies ceased to exist as fighting forces. Many men surrendered, particularly when the Germans promised them food over loudspeakers (a promise immediately broken in most cases). The luckier or more experienced hid in swamps and, if undiscovered by the Germans, survived with food supplied by the local peasants.

Conversely, the Bryansk hexenkessel proved much trickier to seal due to lack of sufficient men, so far more Soviet soldiers escaped from it to fight another day. A bold advance by Major General Wolf Trierenberg split this pocket in two, and the Germans moved to reduce the northern pocket first, using Sturmgeschutz (StuG) III self-propelled assault guns to move through the dense forests near Bryansk and slaughter the trapped Soviets. These low-profile, turretless armored vehicles packed a considerable punch with their 75mm guns, capable of firing high explosive (HE) rounds at infantry or armor-piercing (AP) rounds at tanks.

The Russians fought back with the vigor that might be expected by cornered soldiers, even as the Germans overwhelmed them with better equipment and sheer fighting skill. On October 10th, a large section of the Soviet 50th Army burst out of the northern Bryansk pocket and retreated eastward. Few others from the unit managed to escape after that date.

The southern Bryansk pocket suffered more systematic reduction. Guderian used the hammer of a number of mechanized and foot infantry divisions advancing from the west to crush the Soviets against the anvil of his Panzer corps deployed to prevent their escape in the east. Small groups of Soviets slipped through the tank cordon on October 10th as the trapped 3rd and 13th Armies battered against the Wehrmacht cage containing them, and on October 11th, a massive Soviet attack pierced the defenses at the juncture of the 25th and 29th Motorized Infantry Divisions, enabling many men to escape.

Yeremenko himself only barely eluded capture on October 13th. Though he exhibited a slippery personality capable of surviving in Stalin's psychotically paranoid high command – A.M. Vasilevsky underlined Yeremenko's "ability to weasel his way out, pull the wool over someone's eyes, and his skill at groveling" – the Colonel-General displayed almost reckless courage in combat situations. After suffering a dangerous wound from an exploding shell, he narrowly escaped aboard a Polikarpov Po-2 medical evacuation biplane with advancing panzers only 600 feet away.

October 13th also marked the final end to major operations in the Vyazma pocket as the infantry forces pushing from the west met the panzers and motorized infantry blocking the eastern retreat. Over half a million Red Army soldiers surrendered, while hundreds of thousands more lay dead. Even the Germans seemed aghast at the landscape, carpeted for many miles with shattered and dismembered human corpses, with actual mounds of dead soldiers rising at the points where breakout attempts met concentrated fire.

The battle at Vyazma had an oddly demoralizing effect on both sides. The Germans marveled at the endless hordes of Soviet soldiers, and though they had only lost 48,000 killed and wounded, morale suffered a heavy blow as the ordinary soldiers began to believe they would never return home alive. Meanwhile, the Soviet army and citizenry, aware that the hordes were not in fact endless, felt grief and fear at the colossal defeat the seemingly unstoppable Wehrmacht juggernaut inflicted on Moscow's defensive armies.

Marshal Zhukov took the initiative in stiffening resolve among his men with a widely distributed order sent out on October 13th. Besides lengthy and detailed threats of the deadly fate awaiting "traitors" who fled, retreated, or abandoned equipment, the Marshal struck a confident patriotic note: "Now, in order to offset this failure [at Leningrad], the fascists have undertaken a new adventure – an offensive on Moscow. The fascists have thrown all their reserves into this offensive, including untrained [soldiers] and every sort of random rabble, drunkards, and degenerates. [...] At this moment, everyone, from private to the highest commander, must valiantly and selflessly fight as one for their Motherland, for Moscow."

Fighting in the Bryansk pocket continued far longer than in the Vyazma pocket, but here again a German victory, albeit a costly one, slowly emerged. The combat raged on past October 13th, when the by-then nominal commander of the Soviet forces, Yeremenko, received his evacuation by air. On that same day, the Soviets used the dense forest to close into actual melee with the infantry of the Grossdeutschland Division, leading to a huge bayonet battle in the woodland. The Soviets inflicted heavy losses and killed two men who had received the extremely rare Knight's Cross decoration, and the Grossdeutschland soldiers were so infuriated by the losses that they took no prisoners that day, leaving the forest tracks heaped with mangled corpses. As fighting continued through October 18th, the Russians fought doggedly but with increasing despair, but Guderian's men finally wiped out the southern pocket on the 18th, freeing them at last for a new advance. Most trapped Soviet political officers shot themselves, knowing the hatred the Nazis held for them, and Soviet prisoners who turned over a commissar to the Einsatzgruppen could expect better treatment and more food as a reward. Many wounded Russian soldiers also committed suicide, knowing their chances of surviving captivity approached zero, or they simply asked other men to shoot them. With no medical care available, many badly wounded men gave themselves the mercy of a bullet rather than die in agony over hours or days, sometimes exhorting their comrades to avenge them before pulling the trigger. One recalled, "A lieutenant in command of one platoon, who'd been wounded in the attack, before shooting himself said, 'Tell them, brothers, how we died here, and to take revenge for us!' Private F.P. Chukharev, a radio operator who'd been wounded in the chest, wanted to shoot himself with the lieutenant's revolver. However, the medic Maletsky bandaged him and convinced him the wound wasn't fatal." (Lopukhovsky, 2013, 362).

Around 68,000 men escaped from Vyazma, while 23,000 eluded capture at Bryansk. The rest joined the endless columns totaling close to 4 million prisoners being driven westward. These men, starved, dehydrated, and constantly beaten by the German guards in an effort to make them move faster, died by the thousands on the road. The Germans shot anyone who fell behind, and German vehicles simply ran over any prisoner who collapsed from exhaustion during the march. Nearly 2 million men soon died in German captivity, mostly from starvation and the disease accompanying it.

Many of the men who escaped continued eastward in the hopes of rejoining the Red Army, others remained behind as partisans, fearing that their return in defeat would lead to their execution and the arrest of their families, as per Stalin's Order #270. Many of these newly minted partisans lived only a short time, because the Germans ruthlessly rounded up real or suspected partisans in the following months and executed tens of thousands of them, nearly destroying Soviet guerrilla forces for some time.

Meanwhile, those men who escaped the Germans and rejoined the Red Army forces to the east often experienced another sort of difficulty. Operating almost by the standards of tribal warfare, the Soviets viewed soldiers who eluded capture and fled to fight another day, even from a desperate situation, with a mix of suspicion and contempt bordering on hatred. The Soviets operated by an unspoken but clearly identifiable rule that a soldier who retreated rather than die – however uselessly – at his post, very closely resembled a traitor and counterrevolutionary. Officers who ordered their men to surrender almost always suffered summary execution when they returned home, explaining the numerous officer suicides in units too broken and defeated to continue fighting.

As a result, escapees met with interrogation by the NKVD, and while many escaped this process unscathed, others whose stories seemed thin or whom the interrogators simply disliked found themselves sent to Siberian labor camps where death from starvation, abuse, and disease frequently awaited them.

Chapter 5: The Drive to Kalinin

Even as the battles to reduce the Bryansk and Vyazma pockets still raged, Fedor von Bock used some of his units to push forward towards Moscow, where only ragtag units of militia and NKVD policemen guarded the approaches to the capital, perhaps numbering 90,000 in all. The German engineers, working tirelessly in conditions of bitter cold, wet, and filth, rendered some roads passable by digging drainage ditches alongside them and stabilizing them with corduroy logs, but other roads remained impassable liquid mires.

A picture of a Russian road completely swamped with mud during the operation

A picture of Russian soldiers standing guard west of Moscow

Two Panzer Corps formed the leading elements of this continuing German offensive. The jowly Adolf-Friedrich Kuntzen led the 57th Panzer Corps, while the keen-minded and extremely able Leo Geyr von Schweppenburg commanded the 26th Panzer Corps. Kuntzen's northern push moved very slowly, hampered not only by the mud but by constant Soviet roadblocks. The T-34 tanks showed themselves far more mobile over mud and wet ground thanks to their wide tracks, but while the Germans eventually upgraded their other tanks with wider tracks also, the Wehrmacht had none available in 1941. Kuntzen's column reached Medyn, 84 miles from Moscow, on October 11th, 1941, while Schweppenburg met with poorer success in the south and remaining stalled near Mtsensk thanks to Soviet resiliency. Despite Stalin's ill-advised massacres of his own tank officers, new, successful tank commanders were emerging there through a process reminiscent of natural selection.

Fedor von Bock showed a rather cavalier disregard for concentration of force by dispatching the 1st Panzer Division under Eugen Walter Kruger far to the north to seize Kalinin. Totally ignoring supply and fuel problems, von Bock further stated that Kruger would use Kalinin as the staging point for operations 30-40 miles further north, at a moment when even a few miles' advance often presented astounding difficulties. Undeterred, Kruger's men pushed north to Kalinin on October 12th and 13th, frequently mixing with swarms of Soviet soldiers fleeing along that road from the disastrous Ryazma fight. Lieutenant Colonel Walther Wenck engaged in a bit of drollery when he described the bizarre situation of German and Russian formations jostling for use of the same roadway: "Russian units, although not included in our march tables, are attempting continuously to share our road space, and thus are partly responsible for the delay of our advance on Kalinin. Please advise what to do?' The message was returned: 'As usual, 1st Panzer Division has priority along the route of advance. Reinforce traffic control!!'"

The Germans pushed into Kalinin on the 13th, finding a city utterly unprepared for their arrival, and combat soon erupted. Kruger's 1st Panzer Division experienced a hard fight to take the objective, and the Wehrmacht barely established a marginal foothold in the city the first day. The second day, October 14th, witnessed a heavy German assault from the western side of the town, and the Wehrmacht soldiers, including motorcycle troops, two panzer companies, artillery, and a battalion of flamethrower equipped tanks, pushed to the city center shortly after noon. The Flammpanzer II flamethrower tank crews enjoyed a brief moment of glory as their usually ineffective vehicles cleared building after building and accelerated the advance by panicking many defenders who wished to avoid burning to death.

At 6:00 p.m., the Germans successfully seized one of the Kalinin bridges across the Volga intact; they later found the whole structure wired with explosives which the Soviets neglected to set off. The Germans removed the explosives and set a force to guard each end of the precious bridge. Fighting for other portions of the city continued for days.

The town of Staritsa, near Kalinin, also became a focus of fighting. With its pontoon bridge across the Volga offering an alternative to the two bridges in Kalinin proper (which the Germans feared the Soviets would demolish), the town presented a tempting prize. The German 6th Infantry Division under Auleb moved against it, but they met stiff resistance from the Separate Motorized Rifle Brigade under A.N. Ryzhkov. Ryzhkov held Staritsa until October 20th, tying down an entire German infantry division for a critical week.

In an effort to help hold Kalinin, the Soviets shifted the 180th Fighter Regiment of the 46th Mixed Air Division from Rzhev to the Kalinin airfield on October 13th. The first aircraft to arrive, under the command of a Captain Timofeyev, found the airport apparently abandoned, and when the Captain touched down briefly, a German soldier appeared and fired at his I-16 airplane, prompting him to take to the air again.

Lacking radios, the men could not warn the rest of the Regiment away. Later, the Regiment's head, Captain Sergeyev, landed on the field alongside his adjutant Lt. Klusovich, both piloting MiG-3 fighters, after a skirmish with Junkers Ju-87 Stukas supporting the German advance. The Captain observed some peculiar vehicles, probably SdKfz 250 or 251 halftracks, parked alongside the airstrip. Though Klusovich opened his canopy and shouted urgent warnings to Sergeyev, the Captain walked towards the vehicles and was seized by a truckload of Germans almost immediately. One German rifleman scrambled up on Klusovich's wing, but the adjutant shot the man with his pistol and got airborne again amid a storm of bullets. The Germans savagely murdered Sergeyev, perhaps in reprisal for the shot rifleman, and dumped his body beside the airstrip, where it remained for two months. (Radey, 2012, 59).

Temperatures fell sharply and 8 inches of snow fell on October 17th, exacerbating German troubles yet further. Hitler and the OKW had actually issued large quantities of winter clothing for the soldiers in Russia, but the railways were occupied with moving fuel and replacement vehicles up to the front and shuttling cattle cars full of suffering, dying prisoners back for slave labor in Germany. As a result, most of this excellent gear remained stockpiled in Polish warehouses for months to come.

Before the cold could consume them, on the 18th and 19th, the temperatures warmed and endless sheets of rain fell, turning the mud into a watery swamp. The forces freed by the destruction of the Vyazma pocket pushed eastward again, encountering hastily built but powerful defensive positions near Mozhaisk. The Soviet defenders fought with stubborn courage, but the Wehrmacht managed to finally overrun them in days.

Hard fighting permitted the Germans to break through Zhukov's Mozhaisk Defense Line at multiple points by October 19th, but the OKH (High Command on the Eastern Front) almost immediately began squandering any chance to exploit the breakthrough. Even the overly optimistic Fedor von Bock, commander of Army Group Center, balked at the new schemes emanating from headquarters in general and Franz Halder in particular. At a moment when the hard-fighting soldiers of Army Group Center found themselves exhausted, worn out, hungry, possessing badly battered equipment, and nearly out of ammunition and fuel, Halder concocted a grandiose scheme to send part of von Bock's forces 210 miles northeast past Kalinin to Vologda, while dispatching Guderian 150 miles southeast to Voronezh – all while still planning to take Moscow.

Halder

On October 17th, Kruger's 1st Panzer Division actually attacked past Kalinin – still not pacified after four days of vicious street fighting – in the direction of Torzhok, but after pushing forward 18 miles and traveling approximately half the distance to Torzhok, the panzers encountered such heavy resistance that further advance became impossible. When the Soviets cut the road behind them, Kruger and his dashing panzer crews were forced to turn around and fought their way back to Kalinin.

All the while, both Halder and Fedor von Bock developed a fixation with keeping hold of Kalinin, now rendered utterly useless by the inability to advance against further Soviet pressure. Soldiers and tanks whom von Bock should have otherwise directed to Moscow found themselves sent to Kalinin instead, with orders to hold it in anticipation of a mighty northeastward offensive possible only in the fantasies of deluded OKH officers. Large amounts of men and material struggled through the deep mud of the Kalinin road, subject to frequent strafing by Soviet aircraft, on October 18th and 19th, draining away the strength needed if Operation Typhoon might yet succeed.

Kalinin proved a mortal wound to the drive on Moscow. The attack towards Torzhok cost 45 tanks, mostly Panzer IVs that were almost impossible to replace before spring, and the Germans counted more than 1,000 abandoned supply trucks mired on the Kalinin road, either hopelessly bogged down in thick, sucking ooze, smashed by Russian air attacks, or both. Smaller disasters also struck; an enterprising Soviet tank crew drove their KV-1 heavy tank into Kalinin proper on the evening of the 18th, and these tanks, proven able to shrug off over 75 hits from the German anti-tank guns of 1941, appeared rarely but had a devastating effect when they did arrive. In this case, all attempts to destroy the KV-1 failed as it ranged up and down the streets, running over anti-tank guns and blowing trucks and halftracks to pieces with HE shells.

Meanwhile, to the south, Leo Geyr von Schweppenburg's 26th Panzer Corps remained halted at Mtsensk by repeated Soviet armor attacks using the hard-hitting T-34 and KV-1 tanks. This remained the case on October 20th, 9 days after his initial arrival, and Hitler, the OKW, and the OKH now found themselves in a dilemma of their own making because their numerous triumphalist propaganda announcements of the imminent fall of Moscow prevented them from halting the offensive, fearing that morale in Germany itself would collapse in that event. For his part, Goebbels, the Nazi propaganda minister, evinced distress verging on a frenzy of despair. The architect of thunderous bombast about the conquest of Moscow and the surrender of the Soviets, the small, spare Goebbels now regretted his own extravagant language.

Attempts to meet the soaring claims of propaganda now directly – and fatally – dictated German military decisions during the Battle of Moscow, but on the other side, Stalin showed himself by no means certain of holding Moscow when he ordered the evacuation of certain personnel and much of the government on October 15th. This order caused rioting and looting among the people themselves on October 16th and 17th, as they were understandably infuriated by the apparent cowardice of their leaders after months of forced labor and propaganda calling for limitless sacrifice. With only a vague idea of war developments and news of the Wehrmacht just 60 miles distant, the people's mood turned ugly.

Underneath the immediate disaffection with the Moscow leadership lay a deeper current of anti-communism which the Germans, classifying the Russians as subhumans and brutalizing them accordingly, failed to exploit as they could have. Zhukov already warned Stalin that "half the peasantry" hated communism, and Alexander Osmerkin, a Moscow painter, expressed a similar loathing for Soviet totalitarianism and a tragically misplaced hope in German deliverance: "[T]here'll be no Cheka, and we will have free contact with Europe. I've burned my certificates, cleared out all compromising material from my apartment – the Marxist classics and the portraits and the rest of the filthy Bolshevik rubbish. Good Lord, I think, is it really all coming to an end?"

The Soviet dictator, declaring that he had expected larger upheavals, appeased the populace with assurances of their defense, the reopening of many places of work and business, and resumption of all salaries. The NKVD shot a few persistent looters and arrested approximately 100 citizens (plus over a thousand military deserters), but even their repression seemed low-key. Order returned, for the most part, by October 20th.

As the unrest hovered over the capital, Zhukov and other Soviet leaders worked diligently to prepare the city for defense. The Soviets drafted hundreds of thousands of women to dig 4,800 miles of anti-tank ditches and other earthworks around the city, while other construction efforts led to the building of immense stretches of barbed-wire entanglements, tank traps, and barricades. The Russians disassembled the machinery of over 500 factories and shipped the capital goods east by rail for reassembly deeper in the Russian interior. At the same time, the gulag organizer, torturer, and serial rapist Lavrenty Beria oversaw rigging a thousand major Moscow buildings with numerous explosives, often fitted with anti-magnetic housings to prevent easy detection. If the Germans took the city, these explosives would detonate, quite likely killing many men (as similar experiences at Kiev would demonstrate). Locations prepared in this manner included the NKVD offices, factories, the Bolshoi Theater, the mint, meat-processing plants, trolley and bus stations, railway stations, telegraph and telephone buildings, and even the Kremlin itself.

Pictures of Russian barricades being erected during the campaign

A picture of Moscow residents receiving military training

A picture of the Bolshoi Theater and its protective camouflage

Moscow enjoyed no immunity from German attack despite the absence of Wehrmacht ground forces. Though its airplanes suffered numerous technical failures as the weather grew colder, the Luftwaffe carried out regular night raids against the city, but with 600 large searchlights and a plethora of anti-aircraft guns, plus some early Lend-Lease fighter aircraft from the U.S. and Britain, Moscow's air defenses proved very difficult for the Germans to penetrate. A few daytime raids struck at the thousands of women laboring to build ditches and set up barbed wire entanglements on the approaches. Flying low, these scattered aircraft strafed the workers, killing a few dozen here and there but failing to slow the work due to its enormous scale.

The Germans continued attempting to press forward up to October 21st and 22nd, but the weather made the roads only slightly passable, and the Wehrmacht could not traverse the open fields at all. Zhukov threw every available man into obstructing German progress along the roads, and since they were compelled to follow these narrowly circumscribed routes, German columns met Soviet units head-on rather than bypassing or encircling them. This type of fighting nullified many German advantages, leading to slow progress and heavy losses, while the survivors suffered incredibly from cold, wet, hunger, and exhaustion.

At Maloyaroslavets, on the bank of the Luzha River, 3,500 Soviet cadets were deployed to delay the Germans with orders to hold out up to a week if possible. The determined youngsters arrived at Maloyaroslavets on October 11th and proved impossible to dislodge before the 18th, obeying their orders to the letter. Following two to three days of fighting, the Luftwaffe futilely dropped propaganda leaflets over Maloyaroslavets which read, "Valiant Red Junkers! You have fought valiantly, but now your resistance no longer makes sense. The Warsaw highway is ours almost to Moscow itself! Within another day or two we will be entering it. You are true soldiers. We respect your heroism! Come over to our side. You will receive a friendly reception, tasty food, and warm clothes from us. This leaflet will serve as your pass."

After overcoming incredible hardships and difficulties, the Germans finally reached the end of their strength at the high water mark of Kamenskoye on October 18th, 42 miles distant from Moscow. Encapsulating both realistic situational awareness and surprising humor in a single phrase, the panzer commander Wilhelm von Thoma declared, "The spirit is willing, but the truck is weak." (Stahel I, 2013, 246). The Germans noted that the depth of mud now buried some horses up to their heads if they ventured into it, and it submerged some bogged-down trucks completely.

While the weather itself presented an almost insurmountable obstacle, the Soviets added to the Germans' problems. Incessant attacks under the overall command of Konev – spared by Zhukov's intercession but threatened again by Stalin with execution should he fail – struck Kalinin, forcing the men committed to its defense to hang on grimly to the increasingly ruined city. Other determined Soviet attacks hammered different parts of the Wehrmacht line on October 25th and 26th. These proved better led and better equipped than the luckless masses of men butchered so easily in the summer and autumn campaigns, but the Red Army still suffered from poor troop quality and the deep Stalinist disregard for attempting to preserve human life and thus build up a pool of experienced veteran soldiers.

Divisions arriving from Siberia, freed by the supine inaction of Germany's ally Japan, greatly bolstered the forces available to Zhukov in late October. As Guderian himself remarked in his later writings, "The soldiers wondered at the time why, when Hitler declared war on America, Japan did not do likewise against the Soviet Union. A direct consequence of this was that the Russian forces in the Far East remained available for use against the Germans. These forces were being moved at an unprecedented speed and in great numbers to our front. The result of this policy of Hitler's was not an alleviation of our difficulties, but an additional burden of almost incalculable weight. It was the soldiers who had to carry it." (Guderian, 1964, 138).

A picture of Russian soldiers in Moscow marching to the front

Though the Germans built a railhead as far forward as Vyazma to bring in supplies and completed it on October 23rd, this still left nearly 70 miles between the nearest railway and the fighting front. With mud anywhere from 3-6 feet deep on the roads and the open country an impassible marsh, efforts to bring fuel, food, and ammunition forward proved barely sufficient to maintain the Wehrmacht in place. In the meantime, Hitler and army headquarters both continued to plan far-flung operations to penetrate hundreds of miles beyond the current positions, with no practical hint of how to achieve such miracles.

Heinz Guderian, dauntless to the last, launched a final attack along the highway towards Tula on October 23rd. This highway, ultimately leading to Moscow, remained in better condition than most Russian roads, and it benefited from concentrated German engineering efforts with corduroy logs laid across it. Guderian used his tanks as personnel carriers, thus saving fuel otherwise utilized by SdKfz 251 halftracks for the same purpose.

The Soviets attempted to stop this drive, led by a task force under Colonel Heinrich Eberbach, a brave, snub-nosed man who would survive the war and die in 1992 at the age of 96 after assisting materially in organizing the postwar Bundeswehr. However, Guderian found a weak point, and the Germans punched readily through most of the defenses thrown up to impede them. Eberbach reached Tula, a city of 250,000 people, on October 29th, but he received a bloody nose when he attempted to seize the metropolis from elements of the Soviet 50th Army with a surprise attack.

At precisely this moment, when Guderian just might have penetrated all the way to Moscow from the south, Hitler and the OKW intervened to strip away a number of crucial units for a proposed (and utterly impractical) late-season push towards Voronezh. In fact, on October 23rd, Hitler and his cronies went so far as to order Guderian to abandon his drive on Tula and Moscow and divert his entire army to Voronezh, far away to the southeast. In response, Fedor von Bock, commander of Army Group Center, openly rebelled against Hitler's will for the first time. Appalled and shocked at the nonsensical change of plans, he refused to communicate the orders to Guderian. Making things even more complicated, the OKW reversed its orders once again on October 28th and commanded Guderian to continue to Tula. Such massive, random changes in strategic direction undermined Bock's confidence and highlighted the rapidly growing detachment from reality characterizing the Third Reich's upper echelons.

Faced with impenetrable mud, the Germans opted on October 30th to suspend further operations until cold weather hardened the ground enough to allow a fresh advance towards Moscow. This gave the Wehrmacht men some time to recuperate and resupply, but, as von Bock feared, it also gave the Russians time to bring in fresh Siberian divisions. The German halt lasted well into November, while the days shortened and fighting continued along the largely fixed fronts where the Wehrmacht and Red Army forces abutted one another. A meeting between the commanders of the OKH occurred on November 13th, 1941, at Orsha. This riverside Belarusian city of 37,000, home base of the train-bombing partisan Konstantin Zaslonov and his men, eventually became the site of several Nazi concentration camps, likely due to convenient rail access.

Pictures of Russian mortar and artillery teams preparing for battle

Chapter 6: The Final Phases of the Battle for Moscow

A picture of a Russian scouting unit near Moscow

A picture of a Russian patrol team in a Moscow suburb

With the ground hardening at last in bitter cold, the Orsha conference decided on a double envelopment of Moscow in the approved Wehrmacht fashion. Panzer Group 3 (Hoth) and 4 (Hoepner) received orders to move north of Moscow via Klin, while Guderian's Panzer Group 2 and other elements struck to the south and then east through Tula, still in Soviet hands.

As the Germans waited out the weather, Stalin had taken a calculated risk to bolster the morale and confidence of his people. He ordered two entire divisions withdrawn from the front to provide the men for a gigantic, triumphal parade in Moscow on November 7th. This weakened the front temporarily, but only during a brief window while the Germans showed no signs of moving in any case. Stalin addressed the Muscovites and his soldiers in ringing terms: "The whole world is looking at you, for it is you who can destroy the marauding armies of the German invader. The enslaved peoples of Europe look upon you as their liberators. […] Be worthy of your mission! The war that you are fighting is a war of liberation, a just war. May you be inspired in this war by the valiant image of our great ancestors – Alexander Nevsky, Dmitri Donskoi, Kuzma Minin, Dmitri Pozharski, Alexander Suvorov, Mikhail Kutuzov."

The speech and martial display restored Moscow's confidence in the Red Army and in their dictator. It also achieved great fame in the following months during screenings around the world, but ironically, the film shown did not depict the actual speech in Red Square. The film crew arrived after the parade, since Stalin ordered it shifted forward two hours from 10:00 a.m. to 8:00 a.m., and they initially reacted with visible terror when NKVD men approached them. However, the NKVD and Stalin proved exceptionally mellow and sympathized with the crew rather than ordering them sent to labor camps or killed. Stalin gave his speech a second time indoors while the relieved men filmed him, and the film of the speech was circulated to Britain, the United States, and elsewhere. Thus, ironically, the speech that attracted such vast praise actually occurred in a makeshift studio rather than amid the living throngs of Moscow.

A Soviet propaganda poster that reads "Let's make a stand for Moscow!"

Hitler also made speeches at nearly the same time, seeking to repair the damage the premature October announcements of victory had done. The bombastic lies remained in the minds of both soldiers and civilians, however, and the obvious falsity of the promises sapped the Germans' will to fight, but on November 8th, in Munich, the Fuhrer offered yet another claim of victory after a lengthy peroration in which he clearly made batteries of excuses for the failure to produce an actual victory: "Never before has a gigantic empire been shattered and defeated in a shorter time than the Soviet Union has been this time. This could occur and succeed only thanks to the unheard-of, unique bravery and willingness to sacrifice of our German Wehrmacht, which takes upon itself unimaginable strains. What all the German arms have accomplished here cannot be expressed by words. We can only bow deeply before our heroes."

No amount of backpedaling, however, concealed the fact that Goebbels' thunderous declarations of triumph had no substance whatsoever. At the same moment that Stalin mobilized the patriotism of his formerly doubtful and rebellious citizenry, Hitler's and Goebbels' lies rebounded on them to destroy the Germans' belief in the possibility of winning. Though the soldiers fought on bravely and with immense skill, the poison of doubt and disbelief filled it from the Battle of Moscow onwards.

Army Group Center rolled into motion once again on November 15th, this time over roads frozen hard and fields likewise hardened by the cold. By now, however, Zhukov commanded a much larger force of regular soldiers, numbering some 240,000 men, as opposed to the scratch force of 90,000 militia volunteers and NKVD at his disposal in October. The Soviet marshal, watching the situation closely, launched multiple spoiling attacks against both pincers of the German double envelopment. These met with mixed success, but they served at least to slow the Germans and deplete their already decimated ranks further. "One such attack, by Group Belov against Guderian's right flank, caught the German 112th Infantry Division with no antitank weapons that were effective against the attacking T-34s. The result was a panicked retreat by most of the division on 17 November, an event almost unprecedented in the German Army." (Glantz, 34).

However, the 44th Cavalry Division from Tashkent did not fare nearly so well during their spoiling attack in the north against Hermann Hoth's men near Klin. The brave but poorly led Soviets attempted a traditional cavalry charge against the modern infantry and artillery of the German 106th Infantry Division and died almost to a man amid a storm of HE shells and machine gun bullets. They literally inflicted zero casualties on the Germans, as one Panzer Grenadier described: "We could not believe that the enemy intended to attack us across this broad field, which lay open like a parade ground before us. But then three ranks of cavalry started moving towards us. Across the sunlit field the horseman rode into the attack bent over their horses' necks, their sabres shining. The first shells exploded in their midst and soon a thick black cloud hung over them. Torn scraps of men and horses flew into the air. It was difficult to distinguish one from the other."

Hoth led his Panzer Group 3 (now called the 3rd Panzer Army) against the Soviet 16th Army commanded by Konstantin Rokossovsky and the 30th Soviet Army, between Kalinin and Klin. Desperate fighting followed for days as the Germans slowly hammered the 16th and 30th Armies back and reached Klin on November 24th.

A picture of officers from the 16th Army, with Rokossovsky in the middle

Rokossovsky asked for permission to withdraw slightly to give his men room to maneuver and to counter German outflanking moves on both flanks, but Zhukov ordered him to remain in place. Predictably, this immobility led to disaster. The Germans outflanked Rokossovsky's 16th Army precisely as he expected and seized a number of bridges intact, enabling further advance. The popular, lionized General Ivan Panfilov, a luminary of the defense along the Moscow highway in October, died to a German shell, demoralizing the entire 16th Army further. When it finally retreated, the 3rd Panzer Army swept triumphantly into Klin. From there, Hoth's men took the crossings of the Volga-Moscow Canal on November 28th, securing a path across one of the few remaining major obstacles. Hoepner's 4th Panzer Army, operating in tandem with Hoth's 3rd, reached a position just 12 miles from the Soviet capital. German officers using their binoculars could now see the city's buildings in the distance.

In the south, Guderian had worse luck. The T-34 spoiling attack by P.A. Belov halted his entire advance for a day, and it only resumed on November 18th. After that, the efforts to take Tula bogged the Germans down in a desperate fight at the very end of an extremely extended supply line. On November 26th, Belov led the newly formed 1st Guards Cavalry Corps, consisting of approximately a division of tanks, an engineer unit, and a detachment of BM-13 Katyusha multiple rocket launchers, in a fierce attack against the 17th Panzer Division, routing it and preventing Guderian from taking Tula or advancing further on his leg of the encirclement.

Fedor von Bock's final effort to reach Moscow began on December 1st when he committed the German 4th Army under Kluge down the highway connecting Minsk and Moscow, but the attack came to a crashing halt at Naro-Fominsk, stopped by the 1st Guards Motorized Rifle Division and then broken on December 5th by simultaneous attacks on both flanks by the Soviet 33rd Army.

Seeing the Germans halted in all directions, the Soviets launched a series of counterattacks beginning at 3:00 a.m. on December 5th. By now, at least 3-4 feet of snow lay on the ground and the nighttime temperature hovered around 0 degrees Fahrenheit, chilling the poorly dressed Germans with bitter cold. Still, even as they were forced to retreat, the Germans maintained order for the most part and limited the gains made by the Soviets.

Pictures of German soldiers surrendering

In the north, General Erhard Raus prepared his 6th Panzer Division for the drive into Moscow when the temperature dropped sharply to -30 degrees Fahrenheit, halting his vehicles in their tracks. The Russians launched their first attack against Hoth's leading elements the same day, though without initial success. One German recalled, "At that moment a sudden drop in the temperature to -30°F, coupled with a surprise attack by Siberian troops, smashed Third Panzer Army's drive on Stalin's capital. By building 6th Panzer Division's defense around Colonel Koll's last five panzers, we held off the initial attack by the Siberians, who presented prime targets in their brown uniforms as they trudged forward through the deep snow. This local success facilitated the division's disengagement (Raus, 2003, 90).

Stalin and the Stavka botched their strategy once again, failing to encircle even one major Wehrmacht unit despite their efforts to imitate German envelopment methods. The Soviet soldiers, though brave and tough, still lacked the skill, experience, and keenly professional individual initiative characteristic of their Third Reich counterparts.

That said, the Soviet counteroffensive shoved the Germans away from Moscow and began the slow process of pushing the Germans back further, even if it did not achieve the kind of stunning victory Stalin craved. The retreating Germans destroyed the equipment they could not bring with them, packing tanks with dynamite to detonate them, setting trucks on fire, and "spiking" artillery pieces by exploding charges in the barrel.

Moreover, the weather often hindered the Soviets nearly as much as the Germans, or in some cases more, since the Wehrmacht now fell back towards its own railheads and found resupply progressively easier. Even the T-34 tanks found the deep snow hard to maneuver through, and Soviet air attacks proved largely ineffective. Though the Russians deployed ski troops and attempted the use of sleighs as personnel carriers, these men could not carry heavy weapons and routinely found themselves massively outgunned by the Germans.

The Germans remained formidable adversaries and the outcome of the war in the east remained in the balance for several more years until strategic disruption and Lend-Lease tipped the scales against the Reich. Nevertheless, as machine gun bullets hummed above the snow and the wintry trees shattered amid the thunderous orange bursts of artillery and tank gun shells, by December 11, 1941, the Battle of Moscow proper was well and truly over.

The opening phases of Operation Typhoon – up to the end of the twin pockets at Vyazma and Bryansk in mid-October – had provided the Wehrmacht with yet another stunning victory, and the Soviets lost close to a million men killed, wounded, and captured. A large number of the wounded also died as a result of being abandoned in hostile territory during cold weather. Huge amounts of materiel also fell into German hands or suffered destruction at the hands of the Wehrmacht. The Germans appropriated many Russian trucks, whose simple design and rugged characteristics matched the country's road conditions very well, and while the number of German casualties mounted steadily throughout this period, at no point did it reach crippling levels.

After the fall of the pockets, however, German mobile warfare came to an end. Channeled into mud-filled roadways by sodden pastureland, impenetrable woods, or huge Russian minefields, the Wehrmacht found themselves forced to launch frontal attacks during which the Russians either halted them or slowed them greatly while inflicting numerous losses. The Germans lost thousands of trucks and several thousand tanks, a very grievous blow which delayed the resumption of truly mobile warfare almost indefinitely. With their logistics in shambles and fuel, ammunition, food, and winter clothing lacking, the Wehrmacht were forced onto the defensive and never fully recovered the initiative.

Of course, the largest of the Third Reich's failures lay in the strategic sphere. Rather than concentrating for a massive *Schwerpunkt* to punch through to Moscow and seize it decisively, Army Group Center constantly detached units to open new fronts, take new towns, and launch offensives in fresh directions. Large numbers of men diverted to Kalinin and Voronezh, among other unimportant objectives, drained the strength of the main push and contributed even more than any other factor. Though it's often forgotten in hindsight, the Germans' defeat in the Battle of Moscow was not a foregone conclusion, and the Soviets came very close to losing their capital despite the bravery of their soldiers, the depth of the mud, and the incompetence of the OKW and OKH.

Things wouldn't get any better for Nazi Germany in the aftermath. Hitler took over direction of the war from the General Staff following the Battle of Moscow, and though the Fuhrer actually did no worse than the unrealistic, bungling, arrogant men he now overrode, he certainly didn't do any better either.

Meanwhile, the Soviets mustered new strength, armed themselves with vast quantities of weapons and vehicles sent by Britain and the United States, and gradually overwhelmed the now mostly immobile Germans in a war of attrition, the only type their strategists could win.

A Russian stamp commemorating the 60th anniversary of the Battle of Moscow

Online Resources

Other World War II titles by Charles River Editors

Other titles about Nazi Germany by Charles River Editors

Bibliography

Braithwaite, Rodric. Moscow 1941: A City and its People at War. London, 2007.

Forczyk, Robert (I). Moscow 1941: Hitler's First Defeat. Oxford, 2006.

Forczyk, Robert (II). Tank Warfare on the Eastern Front 1941-1942: Schwerpunkt. Barnsley, 2013.

Glantz, David M., and Jonathan House. When Titans Clashed: How the Red Army Stopped Hitler. Kansas City, 1995.

Guderian, Heinz and Constantine Fitzgibbon (translator). Panzer Leader. New York, 1964.

Kershaw, Ian. Hitler. London, 2008.

Lopukhovsky, Lev, and Stuart Britton (translator). The Viaz'ma Catastrophe, 1941: the Red Army's Disastrous Stand Against Operation Typhoon. Solihull, 2013.

Overy, Richard (editor). The New York Times Complete World War II: All the Coverage from the Battlefields and the Home Front. New York, 2013.

Radey, Jack, and Charles Sharp. The Defense of Moscow: the Northern Flank. Barnsley, 2012.

Raus, Erhard, and Steven H. Newton (translator). Panzer Operations: the Eastern Front Memoir of General Raus, 1941-1945. Cambridge, 2003.

Seaton, Colonel Albert. The Battle for Moscow. New York, 1993.

Stahel, David (I). Operation Typhoon: Hitler's March on Moscow, October 1941. Cambridge, 2013.

Stahel, David (II). The Battle for Moscow. Cambridge, 2015.

Zetterling, Niklas, and Anders Frankson. The Drive on Moscow 1941. Havertown, 2012.

Made in the USA
Middletown, DE
05 July 2019